Is it Fair?

Learning About Equal Opportunities

Key Stage 2 & 3

Written and Devised
by

Sarah Johnston

Illustrated by
Philippa Drakeford

© Sarah Johnston 2002

Commissioned and Edited by George Robinson

Book designed by Barbara Maines

Proofread by Sara Perraton

Cover designed by Helen Weller

Printed in England by The Book Factory, London N1 4RS

Contents

Introduction

The aim of this teachers' pack is to allow children to explore the subject of equal opportunities. Everyone is different, but often being different is the reason people are treated unfairly.

This pack looks at the ways we, as human beings, are different, but also looks at the ways in which we are the same. It enables children to think about these similarities and differences, and see that both can be celebrated. If children can realise that life is more interesting because people are different, and that being different is not something to be frightened of, then they will hopefully have richer and more rewarding lives because of it. In addition, if children can see that it is fun when people are the same, because they can enjoy sharing particular activities, and that people having the same thoughts and feelings about something can bring a sense of belonging and friendship, then this too will hopefully increase the quality of their lives.

Unfortunately, all too soon children learn to think and act like other people without questioning whether what they are thinking and doing is right or wrong. It is only when children and adults are consciously aware of how people are treated differently and unfairly that the world will become a more fair and equal place in which to live. Prejudices against particular groups of people in society, such as women, children, people with special needs and religious groups, as well as people with particular sexual preferences and particular colour skin, still very much exist. Discrimination against these people often results in a lack of opportunity for them to reach their full potential.

In this pack, all the main issues and topics that are important when looking at equal opportunities are addressed, such as prejudice, stereotyping, discrimination and racism. Lastly, the pack looks at what can be done so that there is equal opportunity for everyone in life. It is hoped that this pack will help raise the awareness of equal opportunities. Life should be fair. And being different should be celebrated, not feared.

How to Use the Teachers' Pack

The teachers' pack is intended to let children explore equal opportunities and to see how issues arising from this subject can influence their lives.

Material Suitability

The material is suitable for 7 to 13 year olds, Key Stage 2 and 3. Some of the issues and activities might be selected as more appropriate for Year 5 (9-10 years), Year 6 (10-11 years) and Year 7 (11-12 years).

National Curriculum

The children will be able to practise all the key English skills of speaking and listening and reading and writing. The Gorm Story is suitable for The Literacy Hour.

PSHE*

Personal, social and health education and citizenship are all areas that are addressed in the pack.

Personal Skills

Children have the opportunity to:

"Share their views and discuss what's fair and what's not fair, what's right and what's wrong."

Social Skills

Children have the opportunity to:

"Think about how the choices they make affect other people and the environment."

"Consider the different groups in society and how to get on with them."

"Think about how and why rules are made."

The pack is designed to be used in a classroom situation. The activities in the pack vary from teacher-led discussions to group and pair work, drama activities, and more reflective individual work. The Gorm Story is intended to give the children the opportunity to explore the issues presented in the units in the format of a story, and what happens in a particular part of the story links in with the corresponding unit topic. However, the pack is designed to be flexible and the teacher may decide to pick and choose certain activities from particular units and leave out others.

*Personal/Social Skills – Learning Journey DfEE.

The Equal Opportunities Teachers' Pack is divided into five units

Unit 1:   Being the Same

Unit 2:   Being Different

Unit 3:   Good and Bad Things About Being the Same and Different

Unit 4:   Being Treated Differently

Unit 5:   Being Treated Fairly

Units 1 to 3 allow the children to explore the idea that as people we are both the same as, and different to, other people. Units 4 to 5 look at how being different in some ways can effect how a person is treated.

The lessons are divided into four main areas:

Lead in Activity

Intended to introduce the children to the topic that is to be explored. This can be an optional activity, unless it is stated that it is particularly important.

Main Activity

Contains the key point to be grasped.

Extension Activity

The extension activity provides an opportunity for further exploration of the topic area. Again, this can be an optional activity, unless it is stated that it is particularly important.

Homework

Designed to give children the opportunity to reflect individually on what they have learnt from the lesson.

It is up to the teacher to determine how the activities are used. The accompanying worksheets can be used in a flexible way – for example a homework activity could just as suitably be used for a classroom activity.

Being the Same

Unit 1A

What it means to
be the same

What it means to be the same

Lesson Plan – Unit 1A

Words to use:
same, alike, identical, join,
unchanged, group, majority.

Lead in Activity:	GROUP
Drama Game:	O'Grady Says
Time approx.:	10 minutes
Objective :	To introduce the idea of 'the same' to the children in a fun way

Children must do the same action as the teacher to win the game.

1. The children find a space and stand facing the teacher.

2. The teacher calls out 'O'Grady says do this' and performs an action which everyone copies, e.g. clapping, hands on head, standing on one foot, marching on the spot...

3. Teacher performs a new action which everyone copies.

4. If teacher says 'just do this', performs an action and children do it, they are out and have to sit down. They must only copy the teacher if she/he says 'O'Grady says'.

5. When the children get used to the actions, the teacher can make the changes faster.

6. The winner is the last child left standing.

7. Alternative or extension could be one of the children being 'O'Grady'.

Main Activity:	GROUP
Discussion:	About being the same
Time approx.:	15-20 minutes
Objective:	To introduce the word 'majority'

1. Ask the children what they think being the same means.

2. Ask if they can think of another word for 'same', e.g. like, identical, unchanged.

Use pictures to illustrate the meaning of the word majority. See worksheet – 'Different people doing Different things'.

Give out a picture of a group of people doing different activities. The picture will show a majority of children doing one activity. Ask the children what most of the children are doing. Then ask the children if they can think of another word for the word 'most'. The children can then be asked other questions, either from around the classroom, from other pictures, or by using coloured counters. The purpose is to enable the children to become accustomed to using and understanding the meaning of the word majority.

Suggested questions/activities:

1.   Ask whether it is the boys or the girls who are in the majority in the class.

2.   Ask the children to put their hands up if they own a pet. Then ask who is in the majority – children without pets or children with pets.

3.   Divide the children into groups. Put some different coloured counters on the desks and ask each group to work out which colour counter is in the majority.

Explain to the children that the Government of this country need a majority of people voting for them to be elected. Ask the children what this means.

Extension Activity: SMALL GROUPS/PAIR WORK

Collecting pictures of animals or plants and putting them into the same groups

Time approx.:   20 minutes

Objective: To see that people and animals can look different but still belong to the same group

---

1.   Children put pictures of animals in groups that are the same, e.g. mammals.

2.   Pictures of animals, people and plants. Children put pictures together that are the same, but this time, different animals in the same group, e.g. mammals, reptiles, birds and insects. People wearing different clothes, doing different activities, having different coloured skin, but being the same because they are all people.

Point out to children that people, animals or plants can look very different, but that they all belong to the same group because they are all people, animals or plants.

Homework:	INDIVIDUAL
Writing:	
Objective:	Children reflect on what being the same means to them personally
See worksheet:	Am I the Same as You? The children are asked to write about what they think being the same as someone else means

Examples given might include:

- Same physical features
- Same interests and hobbies
- Same clothes
- Same language
- Eating the same types of food
- Watching the same TV programmes

Different people doing different things

Am I The Same As You?

What does being the same as someone else mean to you?

I think being the same means...

_____

_____

_____

_____

_____

_____

_____

_____

Being the Same

Unit 1B

What life would be like if everybody and everything were the same

What life would be like if everybody and everything were the same

Lesson Plan – Unit 1B

Review of work covered in Unit 1A: Unit 1A looked at what it means to be the same and the word majority was introduced. The idea that people and animals can look different but still belong to the same group was also explored.

Lead in Activity:	GROUP
Discussion:	What it would be like if everything and everybody were the same
Time approx.:	10 minutes
Objective:	To see that life would be less interesting if things were always the same

Ask the children what it would be like if everything and everybody were the same. Give examples e.g. same food, same sweets, same clothes, same television programmes, same computer games, same lessons and every day at school the same (if the word 'boring' hasn't already been mentioned, then suggest it here).

One response might be that a child only likes to eat the same breakfast everyday, or that they would be happy to wear their favourite trainers everyday, or watch their favourite television programme. The suggestion can then be made that it is still nice to have a choice. The children could be asked how many times they have played a new computer game and never wanted to play anything else, had a favourite item of clothing that they always wanted to wear, or favourite sweet that they only wanted to eat, but that they eventually got bored of it.

Main Activity:	GROUP OR INDIVIDUAL
The Gorm Story	
Time approx.:	30 minutes
Objective:	To illustrate in the form of a story the ideas being presented in Unit 1

It is up to the teacher to decide how the Gorm Story is used. The story is intended to complement the activities in the units and to reinforce the ideas presented to the children throughout the equal opportunities project.

The teacher might decide to read the story to the children or to let older children read it to themselves as part of their literacy reading time. The story continues in various installments throughout the units and allows opportunity for many additional activities.

There are questions to accompany each part of the story.

Extension Activity:	SMALL GROUPS
Being the same:	Use worksheet – Five things that are good and five things that are not good about being the same
Time approx.:	20 minutes
Objective:	For the children to be able to discuss amongst themselves the good and bad things about being the same

Divide the children into groups of four or five. Ask them to think of and then write down five things that they think are good about everything and everybody being the same. Give them some examples, e.g. it is good that everybody is able to breathe the same air, can get energy from the same foods, can laugh at the same things. Then ask the children to think of five things that make life not so good, e.g. everybody catching the same disease, everybody in one part of the world dying of hunger, and everything depending on the health of the planet, e.g. needing rain, so that everything and everybody would suffer if there wasn't any rain.

Discuss the findings with the whole class.

Homework: INDIVIDUAL

Writing and Drawing

Objective: Children are given a chance to express their own ideas about Gorm

Give out the worksheet Gorm and Grubgrass and ask the children to draw Gorm and Grubgrass. Ask them to write down what they think happens next.

The Gorm Story

This story is about a creature called a Gorm. Everyone knows about space, and knows that there are millions of stars in space. But what they might not know is that 30,000 miles south of the planet Pluto there is a star which is inhabited by a creature called a Gorm.

I know because I found its diary. My name is F. L. Harris. I hope it won't mind me sharing its diary with you. This is Gorm's diary.

Diary Entry 1: Date Unknown

I got up. Cleaned my tooth. Washed my faces. Looked to see if my new tooth was growing in my other mouth. No sign of it. Fed my pet Grubgrass its breakfast. It doesn't seem to like sandgrass, which is a shame. Had my breakfast - sandgrass. Went outside. No sound, no movement.

No change. Went inside. Thought I heard something. Ran outside. Very excited. Waited, holding my breath. But nothing was there. Disappointed, I went inside. Got out my 'how to build a spaceship in just under an hour, guide and set to work. I've been meaning to make a start on it for a long time. Worked very hard all morning. Had dinner - sandgrass. Back to work. Managed to assemble the engine and complete the tail wing. Tired. Had my tea - sandgrass. On my second mouthful I thought I heard something outside. Ran out. Very excited. But there was nothing there. Went back inside. Felt a bit down. Don't know why. Wish I did. Tired. Grubgrass already asleep. Cleaned my tooth. Washed my faces. Fell asleep straight away.

Diary Entry 2: Date Unknown

Got up. Cleaned my tooth. Washed my faces. Had a look to see if my new tooth is coming through yet. It isn't. Fed my Grubgrass. Shame it doesn't like sandgrass. Ate my breakfast - sandgrass. Went outside. Nothing happening. There wasn't any sound or movement. Nothing changes around here. Went back inside. I thought I heard something so I ran back outside. I felt very excited and I stood there, not daring to breathe. But I don't think there was anything there. I felt disappointed, I have to say, and went back inside. I took out my 'how to build a spaceship in just under an hour, guide and made a start. I've been meaning to begin building it for quite a long time now. Didn't stop all morning. Had dinner - sandgrass. Went straight back to work. Managed to build the entire tail wing and engine. But afterwards felt tired. Ate my tea - sandgrass. Just eating my second mouthfuls when I thought I heard something outside. Ran out feeling very excited. But nothing there. Went back inside. Have to say I felt a bit sad. I'm not sure why. I'd like to know. Tired now. I can see Grubgrass is already asleep. Cleaned my tooth. Washed my faces. Fell asleep straight away.

There are 2,805 further entries to Gorm's diary. All of them are exactly the same, give or take the odd word. All except the last diary entry. I am still not sure what to make of it. I'll leave it to you to decide for yourselves.

Diary Entry 2,808: Date Unknown

Something has happened! Got up. Cleaned my tooth. Washed my faces. Couldn't believe it! I can see my new tooth! Went to feed my Grubgrass. He wasn't there! I looked for him everywhere. Eventually I found him in the garden nibbling on the most delicious looking pink lettuce leaves I've ever seen! And I swear Grubgrass had a smile on its face. Amazing! It's never smiled before. I grabbed some of the lettuce leaves and ran inside, suddenly ravenous to have them with the sandgrass. But when I went to the box where I keep it, it was empty! And next to it was another box. I looked inside and there were these round biscuits. I ate some and they melted in my mouths. Absolutely delicious! How can I describe the taste? Butter and cream and chocolate. I can't remember how many of these mouthwatering biscuits my mouths ate. But the best is still to come. I heard a noise outside. I ran out, my mouths full of biscuit, and I could hardly believe what I saw. There...

Here, the diary stops. I can only guess at what happened next... F. L. Harris

Suggested questions:

1. Why was Gorm unhappy in the first two diary entries?

2. Did Gorm have anything to look forward to?

3. What did Gorm get excited about in the first two diary entries?

4. Why did Gorm get excited?

5. When Gorm wrote 'something has happened!'
   in diary entry 2,808, do you think it was excited or frightened?

Why?

Being the Same

Write down five things that you think are good about being the same, and five things that are not.

Good

1. _____

2. _____

3. _____

4. _____

5. _____

Not Good

1. _____

2. _____

3. _____

4. _____

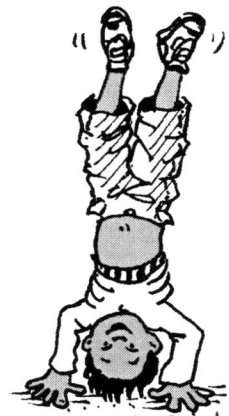

5. _____

Gorm and Grubgrass

Gorm looks like this:

Grubgrass looks like this:

I think this happened next...

_____

_____

_____

_____

_____

Being the Same

Unit 1C

The similarities
between people

The similarities between people

Lesson Plan – Unit 1C

Review of work covered in Unit 1B: Unit 1B looked at what life would be like if everybody and everything were the same. The Gorm story was introduced and the children were asked to think of five things that are good and five things that are bad about being the same.

Lead in Activity:	GROUP/SMALL GROUPS
Discussion:	About Families
Time approx.:	15 minutes
Objective:	To see the similarities in the children's families

The children talk about their own families. This can be in groups or as a whole class. How many people live with them? How many aunts and uncles do they have? If there is a child or children in the class who live in a children's home or in foster care, then they can perhaps be encouraged to write about the family that they might not live with, as well as the people that they do share their home and lives with.

Main Activity:	GROUP
The Human Race:	Belonging to the same family
Time approx.:	25 minutes
Objective:	To see that we all belong to the same family

Write the following on the board or on a flipchart in large lettering:

We all belong to the same human family – the human race

Discuss with the children what they think this statement means. Ask them how all the people in the world can be described as one family. The idea is for the children to grasp that we are all one family because we are all human beings. Explain to the children that all breeds of dog belong to the same family because they are all dogs, just as all types of cats belong to the same family.

The word 'family'. Ask the children to close their eyes and then think of the word family. Give them a couple of minutes and encourage them to really think about what a family means to them. Then ask them to open their eyes and ask what thoughts they had. What kind of things do the children associate with the word family? Ask the children to come up with a list of words or phrases that they associate with the word family, e.g. closeness, support, responsibility, love, being looked after, and being encouraged. Also fighting, arguing, being told off and being criticised(sibling rivalry).

Ask the children to think of a sentence or two to describe the word family.

Different types of families. Ask the children to think of different ways people live in groups: the nuclear family (where there is a father, mother and child/children); single-parent family (one parent and child/children); extended family (parents, child/children and other relatives); communes (groups of people living together who share a common belief or interest e.g. religious groups); a family where there are children who have been adopted or fostered, or boys and girls living in a children's home.

Extension Activity: GROUP

      1.   Drama Activity – The Feeling Game

      2.   Looking at Physical Features

      3.   Collage

Time approx.:   Depends on how many children are blindfolded

Objective: To recognise how much we have in common physically

---

Explain to the children that although people might not look the same or live the same kind of lives, there are a lot of similarities between people.

1. The Feeling Game

The purpose of this game is to show the children how much they have in common physically.

1. One child is blindfolded and turned round several times so that he/she loses his/her bearings in the room.

2. The other children quickly change places.

3. The child has to recognise each of the children (or some of them depending on time constraints) by feeling with his/her hands and recognising the physical features of the children.

Afterwards, ask the child or children who were blindfolded what physical features were the same.

2. Physical Features

Make a list of the physical features of human beings. Write down answers on a flip chart or blackboard.

For example:

1. Physical features = nose, ears, hair, skin, lips, eyes, legs... Next, introduce or ask the children to think of other ways that people are similar to one another.

2. Physical make-up = brain, bones, blood, heart, kidneys, lungs, muscles...

3. Same needs = to eat, drink, keep warm, sleep, to be loved, light, to have friends...

4. Enjoy doing the same kind of activities = e.g. have fun, sports, art, fashion (clothes and hairstyles), listening to music...

5. Same feelings = happy, sad, excited, frightened, angry, proud, love, hate...

6. All experience the same life stages = baby, infant, child, teenager, young adult, and elderly person.

7. Same risks to health from disease = colds, flu, measles, cancer and accidents.

8. Same types of disabilities = deafness, blindness, learning difficulties...

3. Collage

A collage can be started using the statement the children have already discussed.

Title of collage:

We all belong to the same human family – the human race

The children could do their own drawings of people they know, e.g. their own families, their friends, their teachers, popstars and sports people. They could also cut pictures of people from different countries out of magazines.

Homework: INDIVIDUAL

Objective: Children reflect on what their own families are like

Children write about their own families. See worksheet – My Family

---

My Family

How many people are there in your family? Do you have any brothers or sisters? Do you have any pets? What do they look like? Draw a picture of your family.

_____

_____

_____

_____

_____

_____

Being Different

Unit 2A

What it means to be different

What it means to be different

Lesson Plan – Unit 2A

Review of work covered in Unit 1C: Unit 1C looked at the similarities between people. The idea of human beings belonging to one big family. The human race was introduced. The children were encouraged to think about how much human beings have in common physically. They were given the opportunity to make a collage and asked to write about their own families.

Lead in Activity: GROUP

Differences within families of species, e.g. insects

Time approx.:   15 minutes

Objective: To realise that there can be differences within 'families'

Briefly remind the children about the work they have been doing about what it means to be the same. Then ask the children what is the opposite word to being the same. Words or phrases will hopefully come up such as, not like another thing, not the same and/or unlike. The word that needs to be emphasised is the word different.

Remind the children of the work they have just done about the human family. Talk about how within a family of insects, for example, there can be different insects, although they all belong to the same family. On the blackboard write the heading 'The Insect Family' and then ask the children how many different insects they can think of, e.g. spiders, beetles, ants, grasshoppers, dragonflies, butterflies, moths and bees.

Main Activity: GROUP

Introducing the idea of a 'minority '

Time approx.:   20 minutes

Objective :   To enable the children to understand the word minority

---

Introduce the word 'minority' to the children. Ask them what they think it means.

See worksheet – Different Shapes.

Use the worksheet to show that, for example, the picture of shapes with lots of squares and circles, but with only a few triangles, could be described as a picture showing a minority of triangles. Ask the children if they can remember what the word 'majority' means. Ask the children what shape is in the majority. It is important for the children to have a firm grasp of what these words mean.

Extension Activity: PAIR WORK

Being Different

Time approx.:   20 minutes

Objective: For the children to find out themselves how they are different from
                     their classmates

See worksheet – Being Different.

The children find out six different things about one of their classmates. Give them a time limit and
then discuss the findings with the whole of the class. Ask the children whether they like being
different from one another. Is it good to be different sometimes? Does it make you feel special? Or can
it be upsetting? If you are not the same as your friends, might you be picked on?

Homework: INDIVIDUAL

Writing

Objective: For the children to find out how they are different from their families

Children find out what the members of their family like to watch on television and/or eat. Are they
different or the same?

See worksheet – All About My Family.

Different Shapes

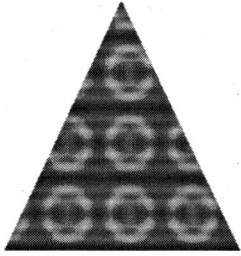

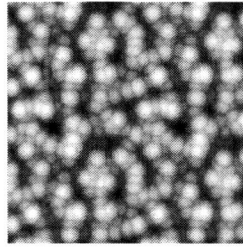

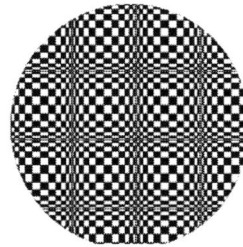

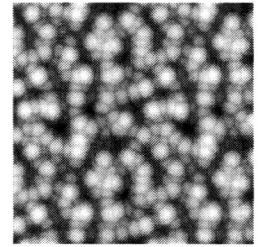

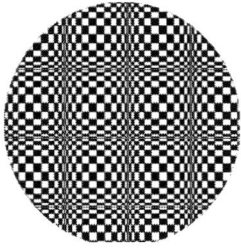

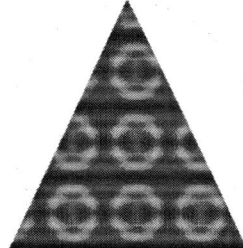

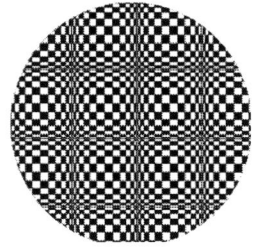

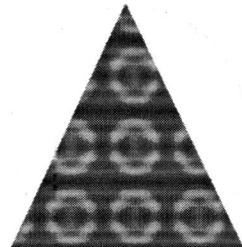

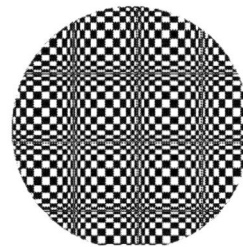

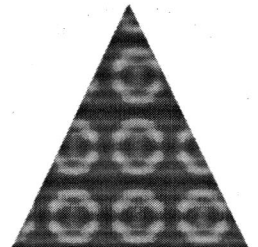

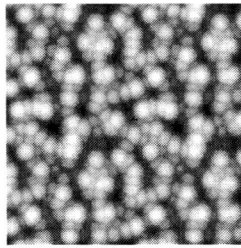

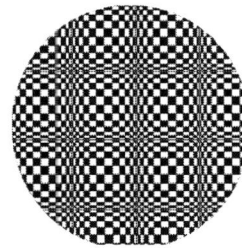

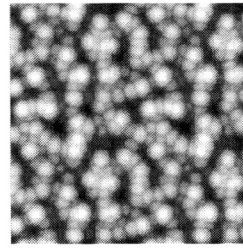

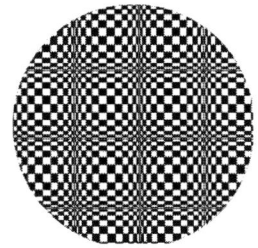

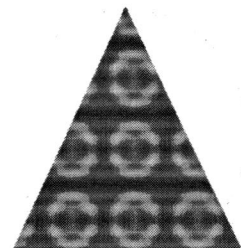

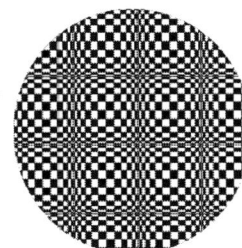

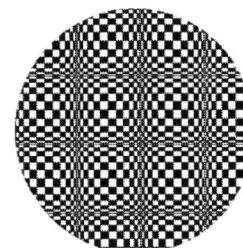

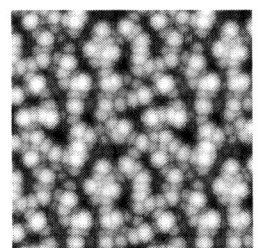

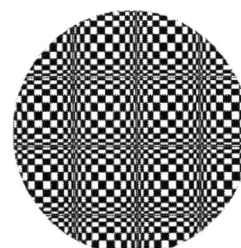

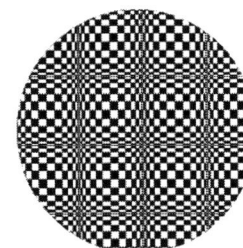

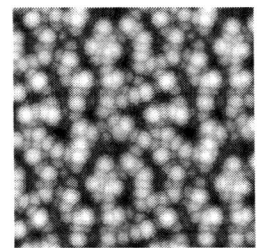

Being Different

Find out six things that are different about someone else in your class from you.

Think about what you look like, what you like to do in your spare time, what food you like to eat, etc.

For example: I have blue eyes, you have brown eyes.

My name ....   Your name ....

I have ....   and you have ....

I have ....   and you have ....

I like ....   and you like ....

I like ....   and you like ....

I like ....   and you like ....

I don't like ....   and you don't like ....

All About my Family

Do members of your family like the same things or different things?

What do they like to eat?

What do they watch on television?

What do they do in their spare time?

_____

_____

_____

_____

_____

_____

_____

_____

_____

Being Different

Unit 2B

How life is changed by people and things being different

How life is changed by people and things being different

Lesson Plan – Unit 2B

Review of work covered in Unit 2A: Unit 2A looked at what it means to be different. The children were shown how there can be differences within the same family. The word minority was introduced. The children were asked to find out how they differed from their classmates and also how they differed from their families.

Lead in Activity: INDIVIDUAL/GROUP

Children think about themselves being different

Time approx.:   25 minutes

Objective: For the children to see that they are all physically different

---

See worksheet – A Picture of Me.

Explain that all humans are different. And that all the children in the class are different. They are unique and special. There is no-one quite like them in the whole world.

Give out the worksheet to the children. Ask the children to draw a picture of themselves. Afterwards, ask all the children to hold up their pictures. Ask whether all the pictures look the same or whether they are all different?

When they say different, ask the children how it feels to be different. Is it good or bad? Scary or exciting?

Ask the children to describe how they see themselves. Encourage them to say how they feel about what they have said. For example, if one child says they are good at swimming, ask how they feel about it. The idea is to begin to introduce the idea that being different can be good, and sometimes it can be not so good, or even bad.

Main Activity: GROUP

1. Different ways of life

Time approx.:   25 minutes

Objective: To see that there are cultural differences as well as physical differences between people

---

The teacher explains to the children that as well as physical differences between people, there are also cultural differences. Ask the children if they know what the word 'culture' means. The children could be asked the question: what is the culture of, say, English people? How do they live their daily lives? What kind of things do they do?

Culture is a way of life, customs, life style of a particular group of people.

The teacher writes the heading on the board – Different Ways of Life – with the following suggested sub-headings. The children are asked to think of as many different examples for each of the different sub-headings as they can. The teacher could choose a selection from the following:

Different Ways of Life

1. Different ways of living, e.g. in towns and cities, in villages in the country, in different places, e.g. as travellers.

2. Different countries, e.g. England, France, Germany, Japan, America.

3. Different languages, e.g. English, French, German, Italian, Chinese.

4. Different religions, e.g. Christian, Jewish, Buddhist, Islamic.

5. Different customs (beliefs/ways of doing certain things, e.g. eating, dressing).

6. Different ways of government, e.g. democracy, dictatorship, monarchy, republic.

7. Different ways of education, e.g. public/private, coeducational, single sex.

8. Different preferences (likes and dislikes).

Main Activity: GROUP

2. The Gorm Story continued GROUP/INDIVIDUAL

Time approx.:   30 minutes

Objective: To illustrate in the form of a story the ideas presented in Unit 2

See worksheet – Gorm Story part 2. The teacher reminds the children what has happened in the story so far. The teacher can either read this part of the story or give it out for the children to read on their own.

Extension Work: INDIVIDUAL

Time approx.:   30 minutes

Objective: For the children to see how being different can affect their lives

---

See worksheet – Being Different

The teacher gives out worksheet. The children are asked to think about how life being different affects them. Discuss the questions on the worksheet with the children. Perhaps write the children's answers on the board, so that when they are asked to fill in the worksheets on their own later, they have something to refer back to.

Homework:

Writing

Objective: For the children to think about how their lives are, at the same time, similar and different to their classmates

The children are asked to write about a typical day in their life.

See worksheet – A Day in my Life.

A Picture of Me

My name is:

The Gorm Story Part 2

If you are reading this, you will probably have heard of my grandfather. His name was F. L. Harris. He found a very unusual diary. Or most of a diary. There were pages missing. He read it to me when I was a child. I always wondered what happened to the rest of the diary. My grandfather had told me he had found the diary in an old second-hand bookshop in London. He couldn't remember the name of the bookshop, but told me the street in London where he had bought it and that there was a weird looking sign above the shop. It was of a man sitting on a moon smiling down at the people on the street below. I am telling you all this because many years later when I was grown up, I went searching for that bookshop and that sign of a man sitting on a moon. I found the shop with the sign hanging above it. But imagine my disappointment when I went inside. There were no books. Instead, there were rows and rows of neatly hanging pairs of socks. When I asked about the bookshop, I was informed that three months earlier the shop had changed hands and was now a sock shop. I don't know why, perhaps it was the kind smile on the girl's face as I turned to leave, but something made me turn back and tell her why I had come. 'Oh,' she had half-laughed back. 'There's a pile of books out the back that still haven't been cleared. If you want to go and have a look, you're welcome. All the decent stuff's gone. There's only rubbish left. All the torn, bashed up stuff and odd scraps.' I hesitated, not daring to hope to find what I so desperately wanted. But I went anyway.

You've probably already guessed what I'm now going to tell you. Yes! I found what I wanted - the rest of Gorm's diary. The missing final pages. And I give them to you now.

Diary Entry 2,808: Date Unknown

Something has happened! Got up. Cleaned my tooth. Washed my faces. Couldn't believe it! I can see my new tooth! Went to feed my Grubgrass. He wasn't there. I looked for him everywhere. Eventually I found him in the garden nibbling on the most delicious looking pink lettuce leaves I've ever seen! And I swear Grubgrass had a smile on its face. Amazing! It's never smiled before. I grabbed some of the lettuce leaves and ran inside, suddenly ravenous to have them with the sandgrass. But when I went to the box where I keep it, it was empty! And next to it was another box. I looked inside and there were these round biscuits. I ate some and they melted in my mouths. Absolutely delicious! How can I describe the taste? Butter and cream and chocolate. I can't remember how many of these mouthwatering biscuits my mouths ate. But the best is yet to come. I heard a noise outside. I ran out, my mouths full of biscuit and I could hardly believe what I saw. There, standing in front of me, was myself. Or at least, that is what I thought at first. But then its faces smiled and I knew it couldn't be me because I have two faces and two mouths and although this creature had two faces as well, it had two mouths on each face, making four mouths in all. Then it came towards me and held out two of its four hands. I was a little scared at first because this creature was not as like me as I had first thought. But I decided to be friendly and put out two of my hands and our hands shook themselves. I cannot describe to you the warmth of those handshakes. I took my new friend inside and we had the most wonderful feast you can imagine. Everything we thought we would like to eat suddenly appeared. We had every sort of pie and sandwiches with delicious fillings. And crisps of every imaginable flavour. My favourite, I remember, was pepper and peanut. Then we ate this enormous trifle with cream piped into enormous peaks topped with cherries.

Afterwards, we sat and played games and talked. My friend is a Gorm like me, but where it comes from all Gorms have four mouths. It says it likes having four mouths because it can eat more at the same time! Then we decided to carry on building the spaceship. In no time at all we had finished it and decided that we would test it out. We don't know where we are going. Another planet maybe, who knows. Grubgrass is coming too. It has made a new friend. Another Grubgrass. Though this one prefers carrots to lettuce leaves so we are taking plenty of both. I am taking some sandgrass seeds in case we find ourselves on a planet where there is no food. We are just about to take off. I am very excited.

Diary Entry 2,809: Date Unknown

Landed on what my friend assures me is a very interesting planet called Cobalt. Lots of things to do and it has good air quality as well apparently. My friend tells me some planets do not have any oxygen which we Gorms need to breathe, so it is just as well we have landed here. Grubgrass seems to be enjoying itself with its new friend. Their favourite game at the moment seems to be rolling over each other at great speed which usually involves them ending up in a twisted heap and I have to go and untangle them. The only trouble is that Grubgrass's friend is twice as big and so I have had to politely ask it if it could be a little careful where it lands. I would hate to see my pet have the life squashed out of it. I have been assured that Grubgrass will not be squashed to death, so all is well and they are having fun and that is the main thing. My friend and I are going time chasing this afternoon. I'm told it is very exciting. Everyone is given a light beacon and you have to strap it to your body and then you just take off. The faster you go the nearer to the time fences you get. If you go fast enough you can jump the fence and go into another time zone. It's very exciting, my friend assures me. I am a little worried as you have to be careful not to use up all your light or you might not be able to get back over the fences. Grubgrass doesn't want me to try it, but I am not one to take unnecessary risks.

Diary Entry 2,810: Date Unknown

A sad day. My friend never returned from the time chasing. The afternoon started off so well. We both managed to jump two fences and went into the same time zone. I cannot describe to you the feeling. It was like being in a massive swirling, spinning rope. The colours were so beautiful – brilliant blues, purples and violets, and the sounds were eerie but sweet and melodic at the same time. But then my friend became caught in the swirls. I tried to help it but I felt the energy in my light pulling me back to the time fence. It was terrible. I waited all the rest of the day and all last night but it never appeared. I fear my friend is lost forever. I have decided to leave Cobalt and go and search for my friend. I have been told there is a planet where lost time chasers end up. I am going to try and find that planet. I have been given the co-ordinates, but I am told it is a very dangerous journey and that there is only a 50/50 chance that I will make it there. I am taking Grubgrass and his friend with me. Who knows, maybe I will find my friend.

That was the final entry in Gorm's diary. At least that was the last page that I could find. Perhaps there were more. Perhaps he did meet up with his friend again, who knows? I have often wondered where Gorm went to next...

James Harris.

Suggested questions:

1. Gorm's friend was different from Gorm in some ways. Did this get in the way of their friendship?

2. Do you think the arrival of Gorm's friend made Gorm's life better. How?

3. Do you think Gorm should have gone time chasing if there were dangers?

4. Do you think it might have been better if Gorm had never met its friend because then it wouldn't have had to experience the sadness when it lost it?

5. Why do you think it was so important to Gorm to find its friend?

6. What does it mean when it says there was only a 50/50 chance of Gorm making it to the planet?

7. Do you think Gorm was right to perhaps risk its own life and that of the two Grubgrasses?

Being Different

1. Being different can make life more fun because

2. Being different can be upsetting sometimes because

3. Being different can make life more challenging because

4. Being different can be scary sometimes because

5. Being different can make life more interesting because

A Day in my Life

Write about a typical day, from when you wake up in the morning to when you go to sleep at night.

_____

_____

_____

_____

_____

_____

_____

_____

_____

_____

Being Different

Unit 2C

The differences between people

The differences between people

Lesson Plan – Unit 2C

Review of work covered in Unit 2B: Unit 2B looked at how life is changed by people and things being different. The children were asked to draw a picture of themselves to reinforce the idea that everyone is different. The fact that there are cultural differences as well as physical differences between people was introduced. The Gorm Story was continued. The children were also asked to think about how being different can affect their lives and how their lives are different and similar to their classmates.

Lead in Activity:	GROUP
Who's the Tallest?	
Time approx.:	10 minutes
Objective:	To reinforce the idea of the physical differences between people

The teacher asks the children to get into a line in order of their height – tallest first. As far as possible let the children see if they can work it out for themselves.

When they are in line, ask some of the children, one at a time, to step out of the line and to come and stand beside the teacher to see if everyone is in the right place.

When everyone is satisfied that they are in the right order, nominate one of the children to write down the names of the children in a list, starting with the tallest first.

Ask the children to measure their heights and to write down their measurements against their name on the list.

If there is a child with a disability that might make this embarrassing or upsetting for them, obviously some similar activity can be used or the activity can be left out.

Alternative activity – the children could get into groups according to the month of their birth starting with January. You can make this activity more challenging if talking is not allowed.

Main Activity:	GROUP
Physical Difference	
Time approx.:	30 minutes
Objective:	For the children to think about the way people differ from each other physically

The teacher tells the children that there are many ways that people are different from one another and that one of them is their physical differences. Ask the children how people differ physically and write the answers on the board. E.g. If they say eye colour, then write eyes, and then write the different colours.

1. Eyes = blue, brown, hazel, grey, green.

2. Hair = brown, fair, red, black, long, short, curly, thin, thick.

3. Size = tall, short, thin, large, round.

4. Skin = fair, dark, smooth, rough, freckly, spotty.

5. Nose, lips, shape of face.

6. Male, female, boy, girl, baby, adult, twins, triplets.

The idea is for the children to see that although we are all the same because we are human beings, we are physically different in many ways. Also, that one way is not better than another, e.g. having blue eyes is not better than having brown eyes, it is just different. Being tall is not better than being short, having long hair is not better than having short hair.

Extension Work:	INDIVIDUAL/GROUP
Drama Game:	One Minute Please
Time approx.:	15 minutes
Objective:	To show that all the children are unique

The teacher picks a child to go and sit on a chair at the front of the class. This is called the 'hot seat'.

1. Child sits in the 'hot seat'.

2. Child has to talk for one minute about themselves without running out of things to say.

3. The teacher times the child. If the child stops for more than a few seconds, they are out and have to sit down.

4. It is up to the teacher how many children are chosen to have a turn.

Homework:	INDIVIDUAL
Writing:	See worksheet – 'What makes me, me?
Objective:	To reinforce the idea that each child is unique

What makes me, me?

What makes you different from your friends at school?

My name is

My birthday is on

I'm me because I have .... coloured eyes.

I'm me because I have .... coloured hair

I like eating

I like playing

I have .... brother(s) and .... sister(s)

At school my favourite subject is

My friends are called

I like

I don't like

Good and Bad things about being the Same and Different

Unit 3A

How being the same can have its advantages and disadvantages

How being the same can have its advantages and disadvantages

Lesson Plan – Unit 3A

Review of work covered in 2C: Unit 2C looked at the differences between people. The children explored the physical differences between people and how every individual is unique.

Lead in Activity:	SMALL GROUPS
Drama Activity:	Being the same age
Time approx.:	30 minutes
Objective:	To see that being with people of a similar age at school has its advantages

---

The idea is for the children to see that children of the same age often have similar interests. Also, that they are at a similar attainment level of learning.

Ask each child their age. Ask the children why they think schools divide children up into the same age groups and teach them in that age group? Then ask the children what they think are the advantages of them all being about the same age. What might be the disadvantages of teaching an 8, 12 and 16 year old together?

Split the children up into groups. Give them about 10 minutes. Ask them to think of as many situations, e.g. sports day, sports, playtime, as well as particular lessons at school, where being taught in a similar age group might have its advantages and disadvantages.

Suggestions:

1. Sports day – if everyone is roughly the same age, then they will probably be about the same height, and this will give everyone a fair chance of winning.

BUT

1. Sports day – if different ages are running in the same race, the older children will probably win because they are bigger and have longer legs!

2. Lessons – if everyone is the same age in a maths lesson, they will probably all have the same experience of doing maths and have covered the same maths topics. That means they should all be able to do the same level maths together. Reading – children of the same age should have roughly the same reading age and should be able to read and enjoy the same kind of books.

BUT

2. Lessons – a 16 year old would be expected to be able to cope with harder maths than an 8 year old. So, if they were being taught the same maths, the 16 year old might find it too easy and the 8 year old too hard. Likewise, a 12 year old's reading would be expected to be better than a 5 year old's because they have had more years to practise. So, if they were given the same book to read, the 12 year old might find it too easy and the 5 year old too hard.

The children could then be asked to improvise a role-play scenario that shows the advantages/disadvantages of not being the same, i.e. different ages in some situations.

Suggestions:

1. **Disadvantage** – sports: one child standing on chair. He/she pretends to be a 16 year old playing basket ball with 10 year olds. One child could be on their knees pretending to be a 6 year old.

2. **Disadvantage** – lessons: teacher explaining a difficult mathematical equation. Children playing older children nod their heads as if they understand, others playing younger children looking puzzled.

3. **Disadvantage** – playtime: some children playing older children talking about who they fancy or talking about what job they want when they leave school. Some children wanting to play in the sand pit.

4. **Advantage** – sport: children of the same age throwing a javelin.

5. **Advantage** – lessons: one of the children plays the teacher and the rest of the children are smiling and putting up their hands because they know the answer.

6. **Advantage** – playtime: all children smiling and playing the same game.

7. The children could be given time to think up their own roleplays for advantages/disadvantages.

The children take it in turns to watch each group. Discuss afterwards. The children will realise that in situations like these, it is good to be the same. However, there will be times in life when being the same will have it disadvantages. To win a medal at the Olympics you cannot be the same as your opponents, you have to run faster or throw a javelin further. In this situation, you would want to be different from your opponents.

Main Activity:	INDIVIDUAL
1. 'Find someone who...'	
Time approx.:	20 minutes
Objective:	To reinforce the idea that being the same as someone else can have its advantages

Give out the worksheet – Find someone who...

The children write down information about themselves and then find someone who has written down the same as them.

The idea here is that people often get a strong sense of who they are by being the same as other people both physically and mentally. It can be reassuring to know someone is like you in some way.

Main Activity: GROUP

2. Physically/mentally being the same – advantages/disadvantages

Time approx.:   20 minutes

Objective: To see that being the same can have its advantages
                  and disadvantages

Discuss with the children the following possible results of being the same as other people. Two columns could be made on the board and the teacher could write the results one by one as they are being discussed. Not all the possible results need to be mentioned and the children might think of some of their own.

Being the same physically/mentally means that:

- You feel you belong

- It is comforting to know you are like other people

- You recognise the same features in others and this is reassuring. It makes you feel you are not on your own

- Other people are thinking what you are thinking, and this confirms in your mind that you must be right

- Other people are doing what you are doing and this confirms in your mind that you must be right

But being the same physically/mentally can also mean that:

- You feel ordinary

- You don't feel special

- You feel frustrated

- You feel bored

- You feel trapped by what people are doing because you want to do different things

- You feel trapped by what people are thinking because you want to think different things

- You don't always question whether what you are doing is right

- You don't always question whether what you are thinking is right

Extension Activity: INDIVIDUAL

Experiences of being the same/different

Time approx.:   25 minutes

Objective: To see that things being the same can have its advantages

Give out worksheet – Things I Like. Ask the children to think about something that they do at home or at school that is always the same, and that they like because it is always the same. Give the children ideas, e.g. Christmas morning, their birthday, their favourite food, their favourite game, favourite TV programme or Sunday meal.

The children write down exactly what happens every time and what is always the same about what happens.

Afterwards, discuss with the children what they have written.

Question: What do you like about what you have described as being the same?

Suggestions:

Good/The Same = enjoy knowing what is coming next, look forward to it, comforting/safe because they know what's happening, done it before so know from past experience it will be OK, fun, habit/ritual. Easier because they don't have to think about it, e.g. getting dressed for school (know what they are wearing).

Homework:

Writing   See worksheet – Things I don't Like. Before giving out the worksheet, ask the children what might not be so good about something always being the same

Suggestions:

Not so Good/The Same = not enjoy knowing what is coming next because don't like it, scary because experience of what happens is not good, boring, no fun, because know what is going to happen and done it so many times – it is boring.

Give out worksheet. The children write down something that they do that is the same that they don't like.

Find someone who...

has the same colour hair as you.

    Name

has their birthday in the same month as you.

    Name

has the same pet as you.

    Name

has the same favourite subject at school as you.

    Name

has the same favourite television programme as you.

    Name

is frightened of the same thing as you. (e.g. spiders, snakes, heights...)

    Name

Things I Like

Name _____

Write down something you do at home or school that is always the same and that you like.

_____

_____

_____

_____

What do you like about what you have described as being the same?

_____

_____

_____

_____

Things I Don't Like

Name _____

Write down something you do at home or school that is always the same and that you don't like.

_____

_____

_____

_____

_____

What don't you like about what you have described being the same?

_____

_____

_____

_____

_____

Good and Bad things about being the Same and Different

Unit 3B

How being different can have its advantages and disadvantages

How being different can have its advantages and disadvantages

Lesson Plan – Unit 3B

Words to use:
disability, deaf, blind, learning difficulty, physical disability, mental disability, barriers.

Review of work covered in Unit 3A: Unit 3A looked at how being the same can have its advantages and disadvantages. The advantages of being taught in similar age groups at school was explored. Also, how things being the same can be reassuring or sometimes boring.

Lead in Activity: GROUP

Discussion about disability – What causes disability?

Time approx.:   30 minutes

Objective: To introduce the idea that being different can have its disadvantages

---

Teacher explains that some people are different physically – not just eye colour or height, but sometimes their bodies don't work in the same way as other people's. They might have a disability that is quite common, like being short- or long-sighted and needing to wear glasses. Or they might have a less common physical disability, e.g. blindness, deafness, a disability where they need to use a wheelchair, or they might have a mental disability, e.g. a learning difficulty. Sometimes people are born with their disabilities and sometimes they have accidents or become ill and are left with a disability.

Genetic/hereditary	E.g. People inherit their disability from their parents, e.g. cystic fibrosis. Down's Syndrome is caused by an irregularity in the cells of a baby during pregnancy.
Accidents	E.g. A car accident – leaving a person with brain damage or perhaps unable to walk.
Disease	E.g. Multiple sclerosis, polio.

Focus on Disability

Having a disability often means that the focus is on the disability rather than the person, e.g. if a person is blind, then that is how that person is described or introduced to people. If someone is blind, then that is their disability, but first, they are a person just like everybody else. They will have likes and dislikes just like you, and thoughts and emotions just like you. They just happen to have a disability as well.

A disability is not <u>what people are</u>, it is <u>what they have.</u>

Social, Emotional and Physical Issues of Disability

There are social, emotional and physical issues that can sometimes make it harder for people with a disability to live their lives. They not only have to cope with the extra physical demands that their disability might create, there are also the emotional effects of having a disability, e.g. having feelings of frustration and anger. As well as this, there are the social issues of their disability, e.g. having to deal with how they are treated by society because of their disability.

People with a disability are often not given the opportunity to fulfil their full potential because they have particular needs that are not always met by society.

But some needs have been addressed:

- If you are blind – you can get special books that have been translated into Braille

- If you can't walk – you can be given a wheelchair

- If you have a learning difficulty – you can get extra help at school and later on when you have left school

But some needs have not been met:

- No access for wheelchair users – there are still buildings and places where wheelchair users cannot go because the entrances are too narrow or there are stairs instead of a ramp

- Visually impaired people – books need to be regularly updated and there needs to be more talking books and Braille books

- Specialist equipment – more specialist equipment is needed, especially modified computers and kitchen and bathroom appliances

If people with a disability are given what they need, then this can help them reach their full potential.

Feeling Angry/Frustrated

Often people with a disability become increasingly frustrated, not because of their disability, but because of how society views their disability.

If someone has a speech impediment because they have had a stroke or have a stammer, then some people are often impatient to take the extra time to listen to them, and the person with the speech impediment feels frustrated.

Main Activity:	GROUP/INDIVIDUAL
The Gorm Story continued	
Time approx.:	30 minutes
Objective:	To illustrate in the form of a story the ideas being presented in Unit 3

Extension Activity: PAIR WORK

Disability barriers

Time approx.: 30 minutes

Objective: For the children to see that it is often not their disability that stops people achieving what they want to do in life, but their needs not being met

Give out the worksheet to the children. Introduce the idea that it is often not their disability that stops people achieving what they want to do in life, but their needs not being met. Ask the children to see if they can think of how the children on the worksheet could overcome their barriers. The children could work in pairs. Afterwards, the children's answers could be discussed amongst the class.

Homework: INDIVIDUAL

Writing

See worksheet – What does it feel like to have a special need?

The children are asked to imagine that they have a special need and what this might feel like

The Gorm Story Continued

My friends, you may remember me. My name is James Harris. Yesterday, I received a small parcel in the post. It was from Jenny - the girl at the Man on the Moon shop in London. I had left my address with her in case she should find any more pages to the diary I had been interested in. I could not believe my eyes when I opened the package. The girl had been sorting out a cupboard in the cellar and found... well you can read it for yourself.

Diary Entry 2,811: Date Unknown

The co-ordinates are wrong. They must be. I have checked and re-checked. But there is no planet below me and according to the co-ordinates, there should be. I am not sure what to do. My Grubgrass is sick. It has not eaten for days. I don't know what to do.

Diary Entry 2,812: Date Unknown

I have decided to abandon the co-ordinates and fly to the next planet. Who knows what I will find there. My Grubgrass is very weak. The other Grubgrass has stopped eating as well. I fear the atmosphere is bad for them. I must find a planet soon if they are to survive. I half wish I had never left my planet. But then again, I will never regret meeting my friend.

Diary Entry 2,813: Date Unknown

I have landed on a strange looking planet. Everything is blue. But the air is breathable, if a little cold and chilling to my throats. Have decided to leave the Grubgrasses and explore the planet. Maybe I will find some sandgrass, or better still, lettuce leaves and carrots for my pet and its friend.

Diary Entry 2,814: Date Unknown

I am a prisoner. I have met the creatures of this planet and they are not friendly. They do not look the same as me. They are blue and have scales and no mouths that I can see. They all look the same. Hundreds of them suddenly appeared. They asked me who I was and where I had come from. But they made no sound and spoke to me through my mind. I told them that I had come in peace and that I was a Gorm looking for my friend who had got lost time chasing. They said I was not like them so I was not to be trusted. I asked them why, but they wouldn't answer me. They repeated I was not like them, but I was different and a threat. I repeated that I had come in peace and had no intention of causing any trouble. But they would not believe me. Then they locked me up. I must escape. I fear for my life.

This was the last entry that Jenny sent me. I am going back to the shop. I must find out what happens next.

James Harris.

Suggested Questions

1. Was Gorm in the majority or the minority when it landed on the blue planet? Why?

2. Were the people on the blue planet in the majority or the minority?

   Why?

3. Why did the people on the blue planet lock Gorm up in prison?

4. Who was the most powerful on the blue planet – the blue people or Gorm?

5. If the blue people were more powerful, why would they see Gorm as a threat?

Disability and Barriers

Just because you can't do something one way, doesn't mean that you can't do something another way!

Can you think of how children in a school could overcome the following barriers?

1. Jemma has difficulty writing because she can't write with her hands.

2. Thomas can't get his wheelchair up the school steps to the classroom.

3. Megan has difficulty talking and so doesn't put her hand up to answer the teacher's questions.

What does it feel like to have a special need?

Imagine you have a special need. For example, you might need to wear a hearing aid or use a wheelchair.

Try to imagine what it would be like and write down how it would feel and what would be the practical differences to how you would live your life.

You can draw a picture if you want.

Good and Bad things about being the Same and Different

Unit 3C

How what people say and do can affect other people's feelings

How what people say and do can affect other people's feelings

Lesson Plan – Unit 3C

Review of work covered in Unit 3B: Unit 3B looked at how being different can have its advantages and disadvantages. The subject of disability was introduced – what causes disability and the social, emotional and physical issues associated with the subject. Also, the Gorm story was continued.

Lead in Activity:	
Drama Activity:	Empathy
Time approx.:	20 minutes
Objective:	To gain an understanding of empathy

The children are asked to close their eyes. The teacher tells them that when they open their eyes, they will all stare at a particular child. They will not speak to him/her, just stare. This can be repeated several times so that quite a few of the children can experience the feeling of being stared at. Let the activity last a few minutes so that any initial giggles and embarrassment by the children doing the staring disappears.

Discuss with the children how they felt about being stared at.

Put it to the children that if we wouldn't want to be stared at then maybe it is a good idea if we respect other peoples' feelings and try not to stare, even if we are tempted to because a person is different in some way.

Empathy

If we try to imagine how another person might be feeling, this is called empathy.

Sympathy is when we feel sorry for someone. Empathy is when we try to understand how someone is feeling. If someone is being stared at and looks unhappy, we can try and imagine how they must be feeling. This is empathy. Empathy is important because understanding how someone feels in a situation means that we might not say or do something that might upset a person if we can imagine how it would upset us.

The teacher explains that sometimes our feelings can be affected by other people.

Main Activity: GROUP/INDIVIDUAL

1. Good/Bad Feelings

Time approx: 30 minutes

Objective: To see that our feelings can be affected by other people

Good Feelings

If someone says something nice about you – for example that they like your clothes or that you are good at something – then that makes you feel good inside. If a teacher praises you for doing a good piece of work at school, then you feel good. If people like you and want to be your friend, then again, that makes you feel good. These good feelings increase your confidence and make you feel good about yourself as a person.

Bad Feelings

If someone says something that is not nice about you – for example that they do not like your clothes or that you are no good at something – then that makes you feel bad inside. If you do not have any friends or your classmates call you names, then that will make you have bad feelings inside as well. This will eat away at your confidence and will make you feel very unhappy.

Give out the worksheet – Good/Bad Feelings. The children are asked to write down what makes them feel good and what makes them feel bad.

Main Activity   GROUP

2. BULLYING

Time approx: 30 minutes

Objective :   To introduce and discuss bullying

Discussion with Class

If someone says something that isn't very nice once or twice then maybe your confidence in yourself will be strong enough to shrug it off and forget about it. However, if the insults and attacks happen over and over again, then this is called bullying.

Bullying is hurting someone else on purpose

There are three types of bullying

- Physical   E.g. hurting someone by hitting them or taking their pocket money

- Verbal   E.g. name-calling, teasing

- Psychological   E.g. staring at someone, sending unpleasant notes, not talking to someone

Why do people become bullies?

- Bullies want to be able to think they are better than the person they are bullying

- They want the person to be scared of them

- They want everyone else to respect them

- Bullies don't usually feel good about themselves inside. This can be for different reasons. They think that by acting tough this will hide their real feelings

- Bullies may be bullied by their older brothers and sisters. They may have parents who argue and fight, so they take out their frustration and confusion on other people

Why do people get bullied?

If you are different in any way, there is a chance you may become a target to be bullied.

For example, you may look different or have a different accent. If you are very good at school work, are new at your school, or if you are very shy, then bullies may target you.

It is important to remember that it is not your fault if you are bullied.

How do you think you would feel if you were bullied every day?

e.g. upset, lonely, angry and frightened.

What can be done about bullying?

If you are being bullied:

- Tell someone – a friend or teacher, someone you trust (it isn't telling tales – it is helping to stop bullying)

- Show that you are not afraid of them

- Best to ignore, not confront the bully. They want you to react to them. Walk away from the bully if possible

How can we stop bullying in school?

Discuss with the group what responsibility they have if they witness bullying.

Organisations that can help

See addresses at the end of this pack.

Self-esteem

Self-esteem means feeling good about yourself. Bullies usually have low self-esteem and that is why they bully someone to make themselves feel better. But it does not really work in the long run.

What makes you feel good about yourself?

For example, having fun, playing with friends.

Extension Activity: Roleplay

Time approx: 40 minutes

Objective: To understand that we have choices about how we react to bullies

---

Discuss with the children the choices people have of how they react when they are picked on or see people being targeted. Discuss the choices below:

1.   Saying nothing – result: the bullying will probably continue

2.   Saying 'no' and walking away – result: the bullying may continue

3.   Telling a teacher or an adult that is trusted – result: the bullying will probably be stopped. But do not give up. Keep telling someone until the bullying stops completely

4.   The role of the observer – what should they do?

It is important to emphasise that the worse thing a child can do is to say nothing, but they are often too frightened to tell

This might be the right time to discuss any bullying that has been taking place in the school or in the class.

NB: This is obviously potentially a very sensitive area. It is up to teachers to deal with it as they think most appropriate.

Roleplay

The roleplay about bullying is intended to let the children see how the three different choices can work.

For the three roleplay scenarios, see accompanying activity sheet: Roleplay-bullying

A final note on bullying

The best way for a child to cope with being bullied is to keep quiet and ignore the bully. The child should walk away from the bully if possible. The children need to understand that the bully wants the child to react. The bully wants the child to be upset or appear frightened. Keeping quiet and then going to tell someone the child trusts is the best way to cope with the situation. The observer should also take some responsibility to do something to stop the bullying. You could discuss why lots of children never tell a teacher.

Homework:

Writing: Children write a story about a child that is bullied at school

See worksheet – Write a story about a child that is bullied at school

Good/Bad Feelings

What makes me feel good?

What makes me feel bad?

Bullying Roleplay

Scenario 1 – Saying Nothing

Characters – Main characters and some observers.

Victim, Bully, Bully's Friend 1, Bully's Friend 2 and some observers.

Playground – The bully and his/her friends go up to the victim.

Bully	Look, it's smelly!
Friend 1	Hello smelly.
Friend 2	Hello smelly.
Bully	You know what we want don't you?
Victim	No.
Bully	Yes you do. Where's your money?

Bully pushes victim backwards.

Bully	Come on, let's have it!
Victim	I don't have any.
Bully	Yes, you do. Urgh! You stink.
Friend 1	Urgh! Pooh! Don't you ever have a bath?
Bully	Come on. Give me your money now!

Bully pushes victim again.

Bully	You wanna thump? Do you?

Pushes victim again.

Bully	Then give it to me.
Victim	All right.

Gives the bully the money.

Bully	Good. See you tomorrow.

The bully pushes the victim one more time and then leaves with the two friends.

The victim starts crying.

The observers discuss what they could do

Scenario 2 – Walking Away

Characters – 4 children, 1 teacher and some observers.

Victim, Bully, Bully's Friend 1, Bully's Friend 2, Teacher and observers.

Playground – The bully and his/her friends go up to the victim.

Bully   Look it's smelly!

Friend 1 Hello smelly.

Friend 2 Hello smelly.

Bully   You know what we want don't you?

Victim looks away. Bully pushes victim backwards.

Bully   Where's your money. Come on, let's have it!

Victim tries to get away but the bully blocks the way.

Bully   Where do you think you're going? Urgh! You stink.

Friend 1 Urgh! Pooh! Don't you ever have a bath?

Bully   Come on. Give me your money now!

Victim   Why should I give you my money?

Friend 2 Because we want it, Smelly!

Bully pushes victim again.

Bully   You wanna thump? Do you? Pushes victim again. Do you?

Friend 2 There's a teacher coming.

Victim pushes past the bully and runs away in the opposite direction of the teacher.

Bully   I'll get you tomorrow.

The observers discuss what they could do.

Bullying Roleplay

Scenario 3 – Telling a Teacher

Characters – 4 children, 1 teacher and some observers.

Victim, Bully, Bully's Friend 1, Bully's Friend 2, Teacher and observers.

Playground – The bully and his/her friends go up to the victim.

Bully   Look it's smelly!

Friend 1   Hello smelly.

Friend 2   Hello smelly.

Bully   You know what we want don't you?

Victim   No.

Bully   Yes, you do. Where's your money?

Bully pushes victim backwards.

Bully   Come on, let's have it!

Victim   I'm not giving you anything.

Bully   Yes, you are. Urgh! You stink.

Friend 1   Urgh! Pooh! Don't you ever have a bath?

Bully   Come on. Give me your money now!

Victim   No.

Friend 2   There's a teacher coming!

A teacher arrives.

Victim pushes past bully and runs to the teacher.

The bully and friends run off in the other direction.

Teacher   Are you all right? What's going on?

Victim   They were trying to get my money.

Teacher   Who was? Tell me their names.

Victim   It was just a bit of fun.

The observers discuss what they could do.

Write a story about a child that is bullied at school.

You can draw a picture if you want

_____

_____

_____

_____

_____

_____

Being Treated Differently

Unit 4A

Just because someone is different, they don't have to be treated differently

That just because someone is different, they don't have to be treated differently

Lesson Plan – Unit 4A

Review of work covered: Unit 3C looked at how what people say and do can affect other people's feelings. The word 'empathy' was introduced. The idea that our feelings can be affected by other people was explored. Also, the subject of bullying was discussed and explored through roleplay and writing.

Lead in Activity:	GROUP
Time approx:	20 minutes
Objective:	For the children to experience discrimination

Discrimination

Half of the children in the class are given wristbands to wear. Those that have the wristbands are discriminated against positively and those that have not got a wristband are discriminated against negatively.

Do not tell the children beforehand the object of the exercise.

As the children come into the classroom, give out a rubber band (or something similar) to every other child and ask the children to put it on their right wrist.

The children wearing a wristband are allowed to go and sit down in their usual places. The children without a wristband can go to their usual places, but must remain standing.

The idea is that various activities then take place that give the teacher the opportunity to treat the children wearing a wristband positively and the other children negatively. Both sets of children will gain the experience of discrimination, but in different ways.

Suggested activities:

Positive experiences – for those children wearing a wristband

- Praised for homework

- Spelling test – praised and encouraged

- At playtime – given a sweet when leaving the classroom

- Classroom discussion – only choosing the children with a wristband

- Use your imagination for other positive experiences

Negative experiences – for those children not wearing a wristband

- Criticised for homework

- Told to stand up for talking, sit still, be quiet etc

- Spelling test – criticising a child, saying he/she could have done better, even if done well

- Not given a sweet at playtime

- Use your imagination for other negative experiences

It is up to the teacher how far he/she feels the experience should be taken to get the point across.

The teacher could make this discrimination a lead-in activity on its own and then stop the activity and explain to the children what has just happened and why; or the teacher could continue with the discrimination, and when doing the main activity about girls and boys and jobs, the teacher could only choose the children with wristbands to answer the questions and mime the jobs.

Main Activity: GROUP/INDIVIDUAL

Stereotyping/Girls and Boys/Jobs

Time approx: 30 minutes

Objective: To get feedback on the wristband experience and to introduce the idea of stereotyping

---

Discrimination – talk about the experience of wearing the wristbands. How did it make the children in both the different groups feel? Explain that the word used to describe how the children were treated differently is called discrimination.

Give out the worksheet – Wristband Report. Ask the children to fill it in.

1. Stereotyping

Discussion

Stereotyping is when a person has one characteristic the same as another person and the assumption is made that they will be the same as that person in every other way.

If everyone over 6ft tall was believed to be bad at writing, then someone who was over 6ft tall and wanted to get a job involving writing would probably be refused. This person would have suffered from being stereotyped.

If people believe in stereotypes then someone will not be judged for what they are really like, but for what they are thought to be like. This is prejudice. To carry on our example, say you were going to have a new English teacher and you had heard the teacher was over 6ft tall. If you assumed the teacher would be bad at writing, then you would be prejudiced against this teacher.

To stop stereotyping, we must not make judgements about people just because they are similar to others in certain ways.

Stereotyping often happens when we think about people from other cultures and religions. We assume people will all act and think in certain ways just because they have the same colour skin or share the same religion. Stereotyping also occurs when people talk about men and women and boys and girls.

For example: Boys like playing football and girls like playing with dolls. Men don't do any housework and women do all the housework.

Even light-hearted teasing such as: 'all people with red hair have fiery tempers' is stereotyping.

Stereotyping is not good because it stops people being seen as individuals.

Stereotyping leads to prejudice and this can cause fear and conflict between people.

2. Girls and Boys

Discussion

In some countries twice as many boys go to school as girls. This is because it is seen as being more important for boys to be educated than girls. The belief is that girls should stay at home and look after the family.

Explain to the children that in some very old schools there used to be a separate entrance for girls and boys to go through when they entered school. The only reason for this was to separate the girls from the boys. Ask the children whether they think this was a good enough reason for having two separate entrances?

In the past, boys did woodwork at school and girls did cookery. Ask the children if there is any reason why girls shouldn't have been allowed to do woodwork and boys to do cookery?

1. Ask the children to put up their hands if they like food. Count how many children say they like food!

2. Ask the children to put up their hands if they like cooking. Count how many boys say they like cooking and how many girls.

Discuss the finding with the class. If there are more girls who say they like cooking, discuss with the class why this is.

Discuss with the children the kinds of jobs they might like to do when they leave school.

3. Jobs

Drama activity/mime

Give out a card with a job written on it to each child, e.g. firefighter, nurse.

See worksheet – Occupations

The children think about how they would mime doing the job. Then individual children are picked out to come to the front of the class and mime the job.

1. The rest of the class have to guess what they think the job is.

2. Then the children have to decide whether they think a man, woman or both would do that job in real life.

Compare and discuss their answers.

Extension Activity GROUP/INDIVIDUAL:

HOT SEAT: Wristband experience

Time approx: 20 minutes, depending on the number of children that have a turn

Objective: The children get a chance to describe how it personally felt to be discriminated against

---

The children take it in turns to go and sit on a chair and be asked questions by the teacher and by the other children about how it felt either wearing or not wearing a wristband.

Possible questions for those wearing a wristband:

1. How did you feel when you were first given a wristband?

2. How did it feel when the teacher was always treating you nicely?

3. Did you realise that you were being treated differently from those children who didn't have a wristband?

4. Did you feel sorry for those children not wearing a wristband?

5. Did it make you feel better than the children not wearing a wristband?

6. Did it make you feel special?

Possible questions for those not wearing a wristband:

1. How did you feel when you were not given a wristband?

2. How did it feel when the teacher was always criticising you or ignoring you?

3. Did you realise that you were being treated differently from those children who did have a wristband?

4. Did you feel jealous of those children wearing a wristband?

5. Did it make you feel as though you were not as good as those children who did have a wristband?

6. Did it make you feel as though you were not important?

NB: If time is short, the children could be asked these questions in a normal classroom situation. They could put up their hands to answer the questions that were relevant to their experience, i.e. whether or not they were wearing a wristband.

Homework: Writing about wristband experience

See worksheet – How it felt

Objective: For the children to have a further opportunity to write down how they felt about being discriminated against. Give out the relevant worksheet depending on whether or not the pupils had a wristband

Wristband report

Name

Were you given a wristband?   YES ☐

                                     NO ☐

Were you treated differently by your teacher depending on whether you were
wearing a wristband or not?

How were you treated differently?

How did it feel?

Was it fair how you were treated?

Why?

Occupations

Nurse	Firefighter
Teacher	Gardener
Doctor	Supermarket Checkout Operator
Refuse Collector	Keep Fit Instructor

How it Felt

I was wearing a wristband in class today and it felt

Draw a picture of how you felt

How it Felt

I was not wearing a wristband in class today and it felt

Draw a picture of how you felt.

Being Treated Differently

Unit 4B

How people are treated differently

How people are treated differently

Lesson Plan – Unit 4B

Review of work covered: Unit 4A looked at the fact that just because someone is different they don't have to be treated differently. The children experienced discrimination with the wristband activity. The word 'stereotype' was introduced and stereotyping was explored to see the affect it can have on the way girls and boys are treated and the jobs they eventually do.

Lead in Activity: GROUP

How and why people are treated differently

Time approx: 25 minutes

Objective: To reinforce the idea of discrimination and to begin looking at how
                    people are treated differently

Discussion

The teacher explains to the children that people are not treated differently just by chance. There are reasons why people are treated differently.

People are treated differently because:

1. They are different in some way from the majority of the people they are living with, e.g. in a country or a town.

2. Their difference is seen as a threat.

3. Their difference is feared.

4. The people in the majority want to stay in the majority. They don't want to lose their power.

5. Some people are used as 'scapegoats'. They are blamed for things that the people in the majority have got wrong and are not willing to take the blame for.

The word discriminate can simply mean to notice the difference between something. There is nothing wrong in discriminating between, for example, different sports, different foods etc. If you noticed the difference between different types of pasta, you would not be discriminating between them, e.g. spaghetti and tagliatelle.

However, in today's society, to discriminate against something usually means that you are thinking that one person is not as good as another. This is unfair discrimination. This kind of discrimination is wrong because people are not treated as equals. They receive unequal treatment.

People discriminate against other people because they want to be more powerful than them. The people are treated differently because they are seen as a threat because they are different.

Main Activity: GROUP/INDIVIDUAL

The Gorm Story Continued

Time approx: 30 minutes

Objective: To illustrate in the form of a story the ideas being presented in Unit 4

Extension Activity: GROUP

Power – Discussion

Time approx: 25 minutes

Objective: For the children to understand the importance of power in relation to equal opportunities

It is important for the children to grasp the role of power in relation to equal opportunities.

Ask the children what they think it means to be powerful. Suggestions could be:

1.   You are powerful if you have money because it gives you freedom to do what you want to do, e.g. where to live, what kind of things to buy.

2.   You are powerful if you have a job that lets you make decisions that affect a lot of people, because you can decide what happens to people.

3.   You are powerful if people will listen to you no matter what your job is, because people will do what you tell them to do. Another way of saying this is that you have influence over people.

People often discriminate against other people so that they can be more powerful. Also, so that they can have more wealth and have better jobs.

Power can be used to help people but also to hurt people.

How people use power to discriminate against people:

- Poor or no education

- No jobs or badly paid jobs

- Bad housing

- Segregation – not allowing a certain group of people to mix with everybody else

- Not meeting the needs of people

Discrimination causes suffering for the person or people being discriminated against. They do not get the same opportunity to do things as other people.

They do not have equal opportunities.

This is unfair.

Homework:

Writing

See worksheet – Write your own ending to the Gorm Story

The children write their own ending to the Gorm story

Objective: To enable the children to explore their own feelings about what should happen to Gorm

---

The Gorm Story Continued

Soon after making the decision that I must go back to the Man on the Moon shop and see Jenny, I fell ill. I have had a terrible fever and have been forced to stay in bed for several weeks. I fear now that perhaps all chances of recovering the rest of Gorm's diary have gone. But today I set off for the shop. I am keeping my fingers crossed that I will be lucky.

When I got to the shop, to my dismay, Jenny was not there. I will have to return tomorrow and am forced to stay overnight in an inn. The inn is opposite the Man on the Moon shop and my room looks onto the street.

As the clock strikes midnight, I am sitting at my window and looking down at the Man on the Moon shop. It is a windy night and I cannot sleep. The sign of the man sitting on the moon is keeping me awake. It is swinging dangerously on its hinges making an eerie, whining sound as if it is trying to speak to me. I know this is stupid. I am just tired and imagining things. I long for tomorrow to come. Will I find the missing final pages to Gorm's diary?

Eventually, I must have drifted off to sleep. It is the next day and the wind has miraculously dropped. There is now an unsettling quietness about the place. There is no other traveller staying at the inn. I pay for my room and breakfast and leave.

The Man on the Moon shop is empty apart from Jenny. I hesitate and then decide to tell her about my grandfather and about him finding the first entries of Gorm's diary. I am pleased at her reaction. She seems to be as excited by the diary as I am. She closes the shop and we go upstairs. In one of the rooms there are piles and piles of old books. These are the books that were thought to be good enough to sell and were kept. Jenny and I begin searching through them. After two hours of searching, at the very bottom of a set of black leather encyclopaedias, we found what we were looking for - the familiar yellow, torn pages of Gorm's diary.

I give them to you now.

Diary Entry 2,815: Date Unknown

Another creature has been put in my cell. It looks very miserable and is huddled up in a corner as far away from me as possible. It gave me an odd look when it came in as though I might hurt it. What I cannot understand is that it is one of the creatures of this planet. It is blue and has scales and has no mouth that I can see. I did notice that it seems to have four eyes instead of three, like the rest of them. The fourth is smaller than the other three as though it has not grown properly. Also, the creature shuffled into the cell and did not walk as smoothly as the other blue creatures do. I feel sorry for this creature. It must feel very unhappy with itself. Poor thing!

Diary Entry 2,816: Date Unknown

The creature has spoken to me! Not through its mouth. I was right - it has no mouth. It spoke through its brain by transferring messages through thought waves to my own brain. At first it was difficult because our brains are tuned into different frequencies, but we have both managed to tune into one another.

The creature's name is Bod. Bod is from this planet and is blue like the others. But it is different from them because of its' eyes and the way it walks. I told the creature I was sorry for it. But it quickly replied that it didn't feel sorry for itself so I shouldn't either. Bod told me it liked having four eyes, especially because the fourth eye could see better than the others in the dark. Bod did admit that walking was not so easy as it was for the other blue creatures, but it could get around and that was what was important.

Bod said that the blue creatures called it the inferior one and that its' mother had been forbidden to have any more creatures in case she gave birth to another inferior one. This upset Bod because its' mother was upset, but it told me the worst thing about being different from the other blue creatures was how they treated it because it was different. Bod had come top of the class once in an exam. Instead of congratulating it they had accused it of cheating because of its' fourth eye. After that they wouldn't let it take any more exams because of its' fourth eye. The other blues in the school said Bod was weird with its' fourth eye and funny walk. They made fun of it. Bod said they were just frightened because it was different from them. Bod was not frightened of them but one blue creature had once tried to poke Bod's fourth eye out with a stick and that had been scary. Bod had fought back, but the teacher had blamed Bod for the fight which was totally unfair. Bod told me that the other blues were OK, but were not very friendly.

I asked Bod if it had had any friends at school. It told me it had, but that its' friend was picked on too because it was friendly with Bod. Poor you, I had told the creature again. But Bod had shaken its' head. Don't let them get you down, it said to me. And to my surprise all of its four eyes went a beautiful brilliant sparkly yellow colour, like fireworks in the sky. It is quite a different creature to what I thought. I like it a lot. It has great spirit. It reminds me of my friend that I have lost. When I asked Bod why it had been locked up in the cell, it told me that it had been blamed for something it had not done. But the creature said this had happened before. Except this time it was more serious. It had been accused of treason! It explained to me what had happened. The blue creatures had found my spaceship and my pet Grubgrass and its friend. Bod tells me they were going to kill the Grubgrasses. Apparently they had left the spaceship and gone looking for food. They had been found in a vegetable patch and had eaten nearly a whole crop of blue cauliflowers. Bod had managed to stop the executions and had managed to hide the Grubgrasses under a large cauliflower leaf. They had then escaped when it had got dark. Bod tells me the blue creatures cannot see at all in the dark but it can because of its fourth eye. I congratulated Bod on its luck at having a fourth eye and how useful it must be. It hugged me and said I was the first creature that had said that to it. I thanked Bod for saving the Grubgrasses. Bod said it felt sorry for them. They hadn't done any harm. All they had done was eat a few cauliflowers. Bod said it knew what it was like to be treated unfairly. I thanked Bod again but am now fearful for the survival of my pet and its friend.

Diary Entry 2,817: Date Unknown
Bod and I are going to try and escape! Bod bribed a guard and has been told that we are both going to be executed as being potential threats to the blue creatures and their planet. It is ridiculous. But neither Bod nor I wish to die. We must escape!

Suggested Questions

1. Why do you think the blue creature thought Gorm was going to hurt it?

2. Gorm thought it was odd that the blue creature was imprisoned. Why?

3. Why do you think Gorm felt sorry for the creature?

4. Why do you think Bod told Gorm not to feel sorry for it?

5. What did the blue creatures mean when they called Bod 'the inferior one'?

6. Why did Bod say it was unfair when it got blamed for the fight?

7. Do you think Bod was right to fight back? What else could it have done?

8. Gorm describes Bod as having 'great spirit'. What does he mean?

9. Why did Gorm think Bod was lucky because it had a fourth eye?

10. Do you think the blue creatures thought Bod was lucky for having a fourth eye? Give a reason for your answer.

11. Why did Bod help the Grubgrasses?

Write your own ending to the Gorm story

Being Treated Differently

Unit 4C

Situations where being treated
differently could be upsetting

Situations where being treated differently could be upsetting

Lesson Plan – Unit 4C

Words to use:
discrimination, racism, racist, superior, inferior, aggression.

Review of work covered in Unit 4B: Unit 4B looked at how people are treated differently. The reasons why people are treated differently were discussed. The Gorm story was continued. Also, the importance of the role of power in equal opportunities was explored.

Lead in Activity: GROUP

PREJUDICE/DISCRIMINATION

Time approx: 20 minutes

Objective: To reinforce the idea of prejudice and discrimination by discussing what happened to Gorm in the story

---

Discussion

Prejudice = What you think about a person (what you think they are like)

Discrimination = How you act towards a person (how you treat them)

Gorm Story Discussion Questions

1. How were the blue people prejudiced against Gorm? (think)

2. How did the blue people discriminate against Gorm? (act)

3. Bod was a blue creature but the other blue creatures were still prejudiced against it. Why?

4. Bod was not only treated with prejudice by the blue creatures, it was also discriminated against. How?

Main Activity: GROUP

RACISM

Time approx: 40 minutes

Objective: To introduce the issue of racism to the children

Discussion

The teacher reminds the children about the work they have done looking at the differences between people.

Ask the children if they know of a word beginning with 'r' which means that some people believe they are better than others due to the colour of their skin and/or their religion. E.g. Racism.

Racism is when people of one race think they are better than people of another race and so treat those people differently and unfairly.

Explain that a person who believes in racism is called a racist. A racist believes that not only is he/she better (superior) because they belong to a particular group of people (race), but that because of this belief, they are usually aggressive towards different races who they feel are not as good as them (inferior).

Racists don't see people as individuals, they only see them as belonging to a particular group.

Ask the children who was thought of as being inferior in the Gorm story.

Ask the children where they think the word racism might come from.

E.g. What does race mean? (e.g. groups of people with similar physical features such as skin colour).

Bod was the same race as the blue creatures, but Gorm wasn't. Ask the children if this is this why the blue creatures treated Gorm badly.

NB: Racism is obviously a sensitive subject and it will be up to teachers and their particular circumstances as to how they proceed with the subject. If racism is clearly evident in their school or classroom, it is up to them to deal with the subject as they deem appropriate.

Explain to the children that racism is unfair and wrong because it is simply not true that the colour of someone's skin, religion or race makes them inferior.

Poem

Read the following poem out to the children, or ask one of the children to read it out.

See worksheet –The Racist. You can use this if you feel that it is an appropriate activity.

The Racist

You are different

You are not like me

You don't look like me

You don't live like me

You might try to change me

You are a threat to me

I don't like you

You are my enemy!

Discuss the poem with the children.

Ask the children to think about what the poem is saying.

Does it follow that just because someone is different they are going to try and change you?

Explain to the children that racism is not logical. It is not based on fact. It is impossible to prove that because someone is different, they will try to change you.

Why are people racist?

Nobody is born a racist. You have to learn to be one.

You might learn it from your family. If they are racist, you might be influenced by what they think.

You might learn it from your friends or your culture.

You might become a racist because you feel inferior and instead of dealing with your feelings, you convince yourself that you are superior to another group of people.

Racists like the feeling of power they have over people they think of as being inferior to them.

Racists like to make people feel frightened because that makes them feel stronger, more powerful and safe.

Racist Bullying

Racists are often bullies. Racist bullying happens in schools. Bullies pick on certain children because of their race and/or culture being different to theirs. Racist bullying also happens to adults.

Racism and Violence

Racism can lead to violence. Different gangs fight each other in street fights. Sometimes the fighting is started by one gang and the other gang fight back in retaliation.

Racism and Self -Esteem

If you are the victim of a racist, at first you will be shocked and upset. If the racist bullying happens over and over again, you will probably begin to feel bad about yourself. You may even begin to believe some of what the bullies are saying about you. Your self-esteem and confidence will suffer.

Extension Activity: GROUP

Racism all over the world

Time approx: 30 minutes

Objective: For the children to explore the issue of racism

It is important that the children realise that discrimination and racism takes place all over the world. There is racism in every country .

Possible examples to discuss with the children:

Racism in the past

1. The slave trade – White slave traders in the past thinking it was acceptable to sell black people as slaves because they believed black people were inferior to them.

2. The Nazis and the Jews in the Second World War. Hitler and the Nazis believing Jewish people were inferior to them.

3. South Africa – European settlers establishing colonies in South Africa and discriminating against black South Africans.

Racism Today

1. There is racism in Britain. Whether it is because of their colour, race or ethnic origin, many people feel they are discriminated against. Many minority groups such as black people and Asian people feel that there is prejudice shown against them by the majority group of white people in Britain.

2. In South Africa today there is much hope that the oppression of black people will end one day. This began when Nelson Mandela became the first black president of South Africa.

3. In Australia, Aborigines are only just beginning to be given rights such as the right to vote and the right to state benefits. The white Australian settlers controlled the Aborigines by taking away their land and putting them on reservations.

Further development – Writing/Research

The children could be given a local newspaper article about a racist incident or watch a television news programme about a racist incident in their area. The teacher could ask the children if they know of any racist incident that has happened where they live. The teacher could ask the children if they are aware of any racist feeling in their area or within the school.

HOMEWORK

Writing

See worksheet: A Bully's Story

Objective: For the children to be able to express their own feelings about racist bullying

---

The children write a story about a bully from the bully's point of view. They could write a story about a girl or a boy who is a racist because he/his family are racists. The girl or boy in the story could pick on someone at school because of what the parents have said. The pupils can illustrate their story or design a poster to highlight the dangers of racism.

The Racist

You are different

You are not like me

You don't look like me

You don't live like me

You might try to change me

You are a threat to me

I don't like you

You are my Enemy!

What are your feelings about racism?

Is racism right?

What can you do about it?

A Bully's Story

_____

_____

_____

_____

_____

_____

Illustrate your story or design a poster about the dangers of racism

Being Treated Fairly

Unit 5A

Ways in which people could be treated more fairly/equally

Ways in which people could be treated more fairly/equally

Lesson Plan – Unit 5A

Review of work covered: Unit 4C looked at situations where being treated differently could be upsetting. The Gorm story was discussed. The issue of racism was introduced. The poem 'the racist' was read and racist bullying was explored.

Lead in Activity:	GROUP
Poem:	The Anti-Racist's Reply (see worksheet)
Time approx:	20 minutes
Objective:	For the children to explore how people can respond to racism

Give out the worksheet to the class. The teacher or one of the children reads the poem to the rest of the class. Discuss the poem with the children.

Suggested questions:

1. What does 'anti' mean?

2. Why doesn't the anti-racist care that he/she is not the same as the other person he/she is speaking to?

3. What do you think 'underneath we are all the same' means? Underneath what?

4. Why do you think the anti-racist thinks it is a shame that he/she can't get on with the other person?

An important point to get across to the children is that it is not enough to know we are the same and should be treated fairly, we have to want everyone to be treated fairly.

Poem - The Anti-Racist's Reply

Just because I'm not like you

I don't care

So why should you?

Underneath we are all the same

So isn't it a bit of a shame

We can't get on?

Main Activity:	GROUP
How to be fair:	
Time approx:	30 minutes
Objective:	To explore ways in which people can be treated more fairly/equally.

Explain to the children that being fair is not always as easy and straightforward as it might at first appear.

In some ways it could be compared to riding a bicycle. When you can ride a bicycle, it is hard to imagine that you once found it hard and wobbled all over the place! You had to practise to keep your balance. In the end you could keep your balance without thinking about it.

Equal opportunities is a bit like that. If you get used to treating people fairly, it gets easier, until eventually you do not even think about it.

There are six important skills that you can learn and use to help prevent prejudice and discrimination. See worksheet – skills that can help. The worksheet should be used after the discussion.

1. ***Empathy*** – this means imagining how others might feel and think in a particular situation. E.g. if you see someone being bullied in the playground, imagine it was you being bullied and how you would feel. You wouldn't like it! And you might feel more determined to not let it happen.

2. **Understanding** – this means thinking about why people are unfair to other people. If you understand why someone is behaving in an unfair way, it will help you to stop it. E.g. If you know Billy is sensitive about his red hair, it might explain why he teases Jane for having curly hair.

3. **Raised Awareness** – this means finding out how people like to be treated and how that can help everyone feel more comfortable. E.g. If someone is in a wheelchair, they would not like to be ignored in a conversation just because they might not be the same height as everyone else.

4. **Sensitivity** – this means being aware of others' feelings. E.g. If someone is a vegetarian and does not eat meat, and you do, accept that person's right to be a vegetarian. Do not criticise him/her because he/she has different eating habits to you.

5. **Consequences** – this means that you should know that everything you do makes something else happen. Being unfair to someone is not good and will result in more bad things happening. E.g. If you treat someone badly, you will have made him/her upset. This is the result or consequence of your action. If you are nice to someone, you will make him/her happy. Consequences can be good!

6. **Wanting to be fair** – this means just what it says! You have to want to be fair. If you pretend to be something you are not, people will know and will not like you for it. If you really mean it when you say something nice to someone, they will know!

Words Can Hurt!

Time approx: 30 minutes

Objective: To explore how what we say can affect people's feelings

Language and Equal Opportunities

People say things that can hurt and frighten other people. Sometimes they are said on purpose to hurt someone and sometimes they are said without meaning to hurt someone, but have that effect nevertheless.

To hurt someone knowingly and unknowingly is wrong.

We need to be sensitive to what might upset someone else.

Everyone is teased now and again, but verbal bullying is different because it happens over and over again, usually by the same people.

The teacher can at this point ask the children to suggest some words that might offend others. A discussion can then take place as to why these words are used and how they can be avoided.

The children can then be given the worksheet – Words can hurt.

Homework:

Writing

Objective: For the children to express their own feelings about racism

The children write their own poem. They can read out their poems to the rest of the class. See worksheet – My Poem.

The Anti-Racist's Reply

Just because I'm not like you

I don't care

So why should you?

Underneath we are all the same

So isn't it a bit of a shame

We can't get on?

What does 'anti' mean?

Why does this person 'not care' that people are not the same?

What does 'underneath we are all the same' mean?

What does 'it's a shame that people can't get on' mean?

Skills that can Help

There are six important skills that you can learn and use to help prevent prejudice and discrimination.

Empathy

Understanding

Raised Awareness

Sensitivity

Consequences

Wanting to be Fair

Give an example of how you could demonstrate each skill

Words can Hurt!

There is an old saying... "Sticks and stones can break my bones, but words can never hurt me."

Do you agree? Or do you think words can hurt you? Write down what you think.

Name calling can be very upsetting. Think of some words that might upset someone and write them down.

Word _____

Why this word might upset someone.

Word _____

Why this word might upset someone.

Word _____

Why this word might upset someone.

My Poem

Write your own poem as if you were speaking to a racist or a bully.

Name _____

Title: [   ]

_____

_____

_____

_____

_____

_____

_____

Being Treated Fairly

Unit 5B

What can be done to ensure people are treated more fairly?

What can be done to ensure people are treated more fairly?

Lesson Plan – Unit 5B

Review of work covered in Unit 5A: Unit 5A looked at ways in which people could be treated more fairly/equally. The poem 'the anti-racist's reply' was read. The six important skills that can be used to help prevent discrimination were discussed and the idea that words can hurt was explored.

Lead in Activity: Group

Equal Opportunities and the Law

Time approx: 30 minutes

Objective: To explore what laws have been made to help people get treated more fairly

Human Rights

The Universal Declaration of Human Rights (1948) states that:

"All human beings are born free and equal in dignity and rights"

To make a declaration or to say something about something is all well and good. But sometimes saying something is not enough. To make something happen or to prevent something happening you have to do something.

That is why laws are made – to make or prevent things happening.

E.g. In this country there is a law that you have to wear seatbelts if you are travelling in a car. This is to try and prevent serious injury if you are in a car crash. If people were simply told it would be a good idea if you fastened your seatbelt, they might do it or they might not. However, because it is the law people are more likely to fasten their seatbelts because if they don't, they will face a consequence of some sort, e.g. having to pay a fine.

Discussion – The teacher explains to the children that sometimes people don't want others to be treated fairly because it is not in their interests.

Laws are made by the government to stop this happening.

These laws are to make sure that everyone in society has an equal opportunity to do things.

In this country, several laws have been passed.

The teacher could mention the following acts to the children.

Race Relations Act 1976:

Says it is unlawful to discriminate against someone on grounds of their colour, race, nationality or ethnic origins.

The Sex Discrimination Act 1975:

Says it is unlawful to discriminate on the grounds of sex or marital status in the areas of employment, trade union membership, education.

The Disabled Persons Act 1981:

Says that people with a disability should be given a fair chance of employment.

The Equal Pay Act 1970 and 1983:

Says that men and women should get equal pay or equal work.

Main Activity: GROUP/INDIVIDUAL

1. The Gorm Story – Final Part

Time approx:	30 minutes
See worksheet	The Gorm Story Final Part and accompanying questions
Objective:	To illustrate in the form of a story the ideas being presented in Unit 5

2. My School's Equal Opportunities Charter

Time approx:	30 minutes
Objective:	For the children to put their own school Equal Opportunities Charter together and so feel that they are actually taking some positive action to ensure that there is equal opportunities in their school

---

The children put their own Equal Opportunities Charter together.

The children could work in groups and decide on five ideas that they would like to see in their charter. One child from each group could be nominated to write the five ideas down and then the class could hear what each group has thought of. The teacher could then choose 10 or so ideas and write them on the board and the children could copy them down on the charter worksheet provided.

See My School's Equal Opportunities Charter worksheet.

Here are some suggestions that the children could include in their charter:

1. Education should be available for all children.

2. Different forms of education should be available to suit the needs of a particular child.

3. My school will respect the rights of every child to be treated without discrimination of any kind.

4. Bullying will not be tolerated.

5. Every pupil will be given the opportunity to learn to read and write.

6. Every pupil will be able to learn about and follow his/her own religion.

7. Pupils will not use language that could upset other pupils.

8. All pupils will be aware that what they say and do can effect other people's feelings – pupils and teachers.

9. The school will provide help for children with special needs.

10. Every pupil should be listened to.

11. Teachers will show respect to pupils.

12. Teachers will not humiliate pupils.

Extension Activity:GROUP

How can I help to make sure that people are treated more fairly?

Time approx: 20 minutes

Objective: To reinforce the idea that everyone can make a difference

---

Explain to the children that sometimes a problem seems to be so big that it is easy to think that one person, especially a child, couldn't do anything to help or make a difference.

Everyone can make a difference.

Here are just a few people who have made a difference.

Martin Luther King made a difference in America. He fought for equal rights for black americans in America. This is because black Americans were being discriminated against by white Americans.

Nelson Mandela made a difference in South Africa. He fought for the equal rights of black people in South Africa. This is because black people were being discriminated against by the white people in South Africa.

Emmeline Pankhurst made a difference. She fought for equal rights for women in England in the early 1900s. This is because at that time women did not have the same pay or job opportunities as men. Emmeline Pankhurst, along with many other women at that time, also campaigned for the right of women to be able to vote. They were called suffragettes.

So what can I do?

Here are some suggestions that the teacher could ask the children to come up with themselves, or the teacher could put these suggestions to the children and discuss them.

1. Take action – do something. E.g. if you see someone being bullied or being treated unfairly in or out of school, then tell a teacher or an adult you trust.

2. Start a group or club at school to discuss how you and your friends can help. Perhaps you know about prejudice and discrimination taking place at your school. Is there anything you can do to help stop it?

3. You personally could decide to become more aware of how you respond to people who are different in some way from yourself. Do you treat everyone fairly? Are there some people in your class that are picked on? Have you ever picked on them? It is hard to ask yourself these questions. Sometimes if you admit to yourself that you have not been very nice to someone, the feeling can be very uncomfortable.

Homework:

Writing

Objective: For the children to explore their own feelings about what it feels like to be teased

---

The children can write a story about a child who is teased at school. Explain to the children that part of the story has to be about a group of children, including the child who is being teased, standing up to the child/children who are doing the teasing.

See worksheet – Teasing.

The Gorm Story – Final Part

I feel I must tell you readers that the next few pages of Gorm's diary are stained a pale green colour. At first, I had no idea what had caused this, thinking perhaps a bottle of green ink had been accidentally spilled on the diary in the shop. But I think what happened to Gorm next explains what the green was.

Diary Entry 2,818: Date Unknown

Bod is badly hurt! Bribing the guard worked and we managed to escape. But no sooner had the guard released us from our cell, then the creature reported to its superiors that we had escaped. An armed guard of 20 or more of these horrible creatures were sent after us.

Fortunately, we managed to lose them by hiding under a big rock. But Bod was speared in the arm by one of the guards as we made our escape, and the arm is bleeding badly. I am not sure what to do. Bod tells me that I must leave it. That it is dying. I don't know if Bod is just saying this so that I can go quicker without it. The creature is losing a lot of blood from its arm – if it is blood – it is not blue like my blood but green. Anyway, whatever the green liquid is, it is draining my friend's life away.

I will stay with Bod. I couldn't bear to lose another friend and I will not leave it to be found by the guards. I hate to imagine what they would do to it.

Diary Entry 2,819: Date Unknown

We have made it to the space ship. It is still safe. I cannot believe our luck that it has not been found. But the Grubgrasses are nowhere to be seen. I have searched everywhere – all over the space ship and in the surrounding countryside. Nothing. The Grubgrasss must be dead.

Diary Entry 2,820: Date Unknown

My heart is heavy. One of the guards of this loathsome planet spotted me by the river this morning searching for the Grubgrasses. It is only a matter of time now before the space ship is discovered. I have made a decision. I must leave my beloved Grubgrass and his friend and escape from this planet while I can.

Diary Entry 2821: Date Unknown

Bod and I have been travelling for three days now. No planet is in sight. I have programmed the ship's computer to search out co-ordinates that will take us to the nearest planet. Bod has been very quiet. The creature's arm is no longer oozing the green liquid. The skin is already healing itself – tiny scale like squares have appeared over the wound. I feel an empty ache inside for the loss of my Grubgrass.

Diary Entry 2,822: Date Unknown

A planet! It is orange and shaped like a tyre with a hole in the middle of it. Bod and I have decided to take our chances and land on this strange looking planet.

Diary Entry 2,823: Date Unknown

I wish that any of you who are reading this diary could be here with me now. I think I may have dreamed of such a place in my sleep. But, oh, my friend – if only you could be here. It is so beautiful.

As we descended into this planet's atmosphere, we were sucked into a warming, orange glow of light. I can only describe it as similar to a warm pool of water that makes you feel so relaxed and happy you could fall asleep and know you wouldn't have any nightmares.

Everything is orange. But if you can imagine 100 shades of orange at the same time rippling in and out of each other – then that is the colour of this planet.

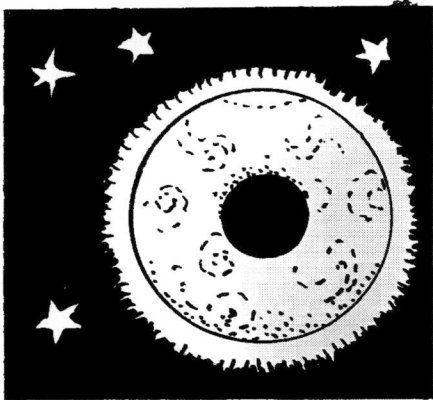

The people are orange. They are called Otans. They have mouths the shape of their planet, lips completely circular, never changing shape. Their voice – sweet and calm – appears to float like an orange mist from the hole in the middle.

And they are so friendly! As we began to land, 100, no probably thousands of the creatures, only as tall as my waist, bobbed their round heads at us. Their eyes were shining with warmth. We were carried like gods to a large arena and three of the Otans bought us food and drink. Round rings of different orange shaped food, tasting of cream and custard and chocolate. Apparently we are the Otans' first visitors in 3000 years.

Diary Entry 2,824: Date Unknown

We have been on this planet for 12 days now. Bod is much better and we are preparing to leave. The Otans have heard about time travelling and have given us new co-ordinates for the planet where my time travelling friend might be.

The Otans have been so helpful and could not be more different than the creatures on Bod's planet. Here there is no war. No prisons. The planet is ruled by all the people and run by an elected group of Otans called 'The Listeners'. Every 100 Otans elect a Listener to represent them. No one is seen as being more important than anyone else. A virus that infected the planet 500 years ago left some of the Otans a pale yellow colour instead of the rich orange of the majority of the creatures. But these minority Otans are treated no differently from the other Otans.

Diary Entry 2,825: Date Unknown

Sadly, it is time to leave the planet Otan. Bod and I have made so many friends and we have been invited to stay for as long as we want. But the Otans understand that I want to find my time travelling friend. We leave tomorrow.

Diary Entry 2,826: Date Unknown

We are not leaving today after all! So much has happened. I can hardly bring myself to write in my diary. I am so happy. I am sure you would never be able to guess who is sitting beside me now. My beloved Grubgrass! This morning I went into my spaceship to try and find something that I could give as a present to the Otans as a thank you for their hospitality. I couldn't think of anything and then I suddenly remembered the seeds of sandgrass that I had brought from my own planet.

I went to where I had put the seeds, which was in a dark corner of the spaceship under the engine where they would have been kept dry and out of the light. I hadn't been in this part of the ship since I had left my own planet and certainly had not thought to search here for the Grubrasses. As I got to the place, I had noticed that some boxes had fallen on top of the sack of seeds. I didn't think much about it. But as I lifted one of the boxes, I heard a tiny gasp. I quickly dragged away the second box and there underneath it were two very thin and very squashed Grubgrasses. I cried out in delight and lifted the poor creatures up. The starving creatures had obviously been trying to get to the sandgrass and dislodged the boxes which had fallen on top of them trapping them!

Diary Entry 2,827: Date Unknown

We leave today. The Grubgrasses haven't stopped eating since they were found and are fat and happy. I cannot believe I never thought to look in that part of the ship for them. But my Grubgrass does not seem to be cross with me. The Otans are delighted with their sandgrass seeds and do not seem to mind that the sandgrass is blue and not orange. In fact they said it would be nice to have a different colour food to eat for a change. Everything is good. Bod is well now. My Grubgrass and the other Grubgrass have never looked so healthy. I am happy. But something inside me says that I must try and find my time-traveller friend. After all, it was because of my friend that I dared to leave my planet. If I hadn't, I would not have met all my new friends and have had all the adventures I have had. I don't know where I will be when I next write in my diary. Another planet? Who knows?

Some important ideas in the story.

1. How did the creatures on the planet Otan treat Gorm differently from the creatures on Bod's planet?

2. Who treated Gorm and Bod more fairly? The Otans or the creatures on Bod's planet?

3. How did the creatures of Otan make sure that everyone was treated fairly?

4. What laws did the Otans have that helped to make sure that they were all treated fairly?

My School's Equal Opportunities Charter

_____

_____

_____

_____

_____

_____

_____

_____

_____

Teasing

Write a story about somebody who is being teased and called names at school.

Include in your story what other children can do to help the target of the teasing.

This is what was happening...

_____

_____

_____

_____

_____

_____

And this is what can be done...

_____

_____

_____

_____

_____

_____

Being Treated Fairly

Unit 5C

What has been learned while doing the project?

What has been learned while doing the project?

Lesson Plan – Unit 5C

Review of work covered in Unit 5B: Unit 5B looked at what can be done to help people be treated more fairly. The issue of human rights was introduced. Laws made to promote equal opportunities were looked at. There was the final part of the Gorm story. Making a school equal opportunities Charter was suggested. The children also looked at what they themselves could do to help establish Equal Opportunities both in and out of school.

Lead in Activity: GROUP

Discussion: What have I learnt about Equal Opportunities?

Time approx: 20 minutes

Objective: For the children to think about what they have learnt about equal opportunities

---

The teacher discusses with the children what the equal opportunities project has been about, and what they have learnt about equal opportunities.

The teacher can ask the children what parts of the project they have enjoyed the most.

Main Activity: GROUP/INDIVIDUAL

Awareness not Ignorance

Time approx: 25 minutes

Objective: For the children to think about what they have personally learnt about equal opportunities

---

The teacher discusses with the children that now they know about equal opportunities they are aware of how life can be unfair if people are not given an equal opportunity or chance to do things that others might take for granted. Some people do not think – or choose not to think – about equal opportunities. This can be described as ignorance.

What I know about equal opportunities

The teacher discusses with the children the meanings of the new words they have learnt while they have been doing the equal Oopportunities project. The words can be written on the board or on a projection system.

Give out the worksheet – What I know about Equal Opportunities.

Extension Activity

Equal Opportunities: Don't forget the opportunity part!

Time approx: 15 minutes

Objective: To introduce the idea that equal opportunities is also about people reaching their potential in life

---

The teacher explains to the children that equal opportunities is not just about stopping people being called names and making sure people are not prevented from doing certain things because of their race, religion or sex. It is also to do with being the best you can and not letting anything stand in your way. It does not matter where you come from or what people say you can and can't do.

E.g. You might want to grow up to be an astronaut. If your parents were both astronauts or you come from a long line of astronauts, then it would be easier for you to imagine yourself being one. But if your family and friends had never even thought of being an astronaut, then they might think it odd you wanting to be one, and may try to put you off the idea!

Equal opportunities is not just about everyone being treated fairly, but is also about everyone reaching their full potential. Decide what you want to do in life and go and do it. There will be help for you somewhere, but you have to go and find it!

Homework:

Writing

Children write about what they want to be when they grow up

Objective: For the children to think about what they want to do with their lives.
                     See worksheet – When I grow up I'm going to

---

What I Know about Equal Opportunities

1. Equal Opportunities means

2. Fairness means

3. Prejudice means

4. Discrimination means

5. Stereotype means

6. Empathy means

When I grow up I'm going to...

Addresses for Further Information

Amnesty International
St. Ives House
99-119 Rosebery Avenue
London
EC1R 4RE
Tel: 020 7814 6200

Anti-Bullying Campaign
18 Elmgate Gardens
Edgware
Middlesex
HA8 9RT
Tel: 020 7378 1446

Childline
Studd Street
London
N1 OQW
Tel: 0800 1111

The Commission for Racial Equality
Head Office
Elliot House
10 –12 Allington Street
London
SW1E 5EF
Tel: 020 7828 7022

Council for Disabled Children
C/o National Children's Bureau
8 Wakley Street
London
EC1V 7QE
Tel: 020 7843 6000

Equal Opportunities Commission
Arndale House
Arndale Centre
Manchester
M4 3AQ
Tel: 0161 833 9244

Kidscape Children's Charity
2 Grosvenor Gardens
London
SW1 WODH
Tel: 020 7730 3300

Mencap
123 Golden Lane
London
EC1Y ORT
Tel: 020 7454 0454